Toolkit for Parents

"BE YOUR CHILD'S ENCOURAGEMENT"

Help Your Child With Speech Therapy

Copyright © 2022 by William Orwell - All rights reserved.

No portion of this book may be reproduced in any form without written permission from the publisher or author, except as permitted by U.S. copyright law.

This publication is designed to provide accurate and authoritative information in regard to the subject matter covered. It is sold with the understanding that neither the author nor the publisher is engaged in rendering legal, investment, accounting or other professional services. While the publisher and author have used their best efforts in preparing this book, they make no representations or warranties with respect to the accuracy or completeness of the contents of this book and specifically disclaim any implied warranties of merchantability or fitness for a particular purpose. This book also contains affiliate links, which means that if you use one of the product links, we'll receive a small commission. This helps support the project and allows us to continue to make books and other content like this. Thank you for the support.

No warranty may be created or extended by sales representatives or written sales materials. The advice and strategies contained herein may not be suitable for your situation. You should consult with a professional when appropriate. Neither the publisher nor the author shall be liable for any loss of profit or any other commercial damages, including but not limited to special, incidental, consequential, personal, or other damages.

Book Publishing & Marketing Assistance by Digimasterz.net

FREE GOODIES FOR OUR DEAR READERS

Congratulations! You are eligible for free coloring books, self-organizing planner and many more gifts. Get Free Goodies, free books and many more surprises by connecting with us.

Just email us at: info@hafizpublications.com

Or Visit us at hafizpublications.com

Table of Contents

Let Us Help You Understand Your Kid   6

    12 Early Signs That Your Child Is Suffering from A Speech Disorder   6

    Checklist of warning signs related to speech disorders   7

    Will My Child's Speech Problems Be Overcome? 13

Time For Parents To Help Their Children, More Power To You All   20

    Different Strategies For Speech Therapy That Parents Can Employ At Home   20

Make Homeschooling For Children With Autism Enjoyable And Effective   34

    Include Activities and Subjects Which Motivate Them To Learn   38

    22 Things To Help Your Children With Speech Disorders Gain Confidence   41

Make Your Autistic Kid A Fluent Speaker   51

    How To Keep Your Child Committed To Meet His Speech Standards?   56

Activities And Games To Aid At Home Speech Therapy   61

    School Going Speech Therapy Games   64

8 Ways Of Technology To Help Home-Based Speech Therapy	66
Developing Pretend Plays As Effective Speech Therapy Techniques	72
Playing Ideas For Your Little Ones	75
Epilogue	80

Let Us Help You Understand Your Kid

12 Early Signs That Your Child Is Suffering from A Speech Disorder

In everyone's view, their child is flawless. While it may be challenging to look past this, you will have to do so to reach speech and language milestones for the sake of your child. If your child is under the age of three, there are some critical things to go through if you are concerned with their speech problems.

- Does your kid appear to be deafening?
- Has your kid begun to utter words?
- Does your child cry a lot or throw tantrums?

If you responded yes to any of these questions, your kid might be displaying indications of speech issues.

It's important to remember that each kid develops at their speed, but it's also essential to think about their developmental milestones. Unfortunately, few parents still use the "wait and see" strategy.

If your kid is already displaying indications of speech delay, we recommend helping your kid with at-home speech therapy activities.

Some of the common symptoms of a speech problem include:

- Mispronounces the letters p, b, m, h, and w (1–2 years)
- Produces muddled speech, especially when speaking to known persons (2–3 years)
- Repetition of beginning sounds of words (ages 2–3)
- Difficulties saying sounds or words (2–3 years)
- Mispronounces the letters k, g, f, t, d, and n (2–3 years)
- Extends sounds (2–3 years)
- Talks with a lot of pauses (2–3 years)
- Speaks in a nasal tone.
- Speaks with a harsh or breathy tone

Checklist of warning signs related to speech disorders

Use our speech development checklist to assess your child

1. **Your Child Doesn't Speak**

If your 7-month-old isn't babbling yet, you should consult your physician to see if they have any deficiencies, including hearing and speech difficulties.

2. Lack Of Group Participation In Your Kid

Speech and language difficulties, as well as social communication problems, are common in children with autism. Early identification of this problem is now possible thanks to modern medical technology, which allows for early intervention.

Early speech therapy at home can help your kid develop the abilities they need to participate in social interactions and establish friends at school.

3. Your Child Has A Stuttering Problem

If your child has a stuttering issue, then they may be starting to stutter by the age of 2 years. Stuttering might look like normal disfluency in children, although it is more common. For example, before pronouncing a word, they may repeat entire syllables, one syllable, or block entirely. But no worries, parents! Your child is normal as every other kid; you just need to put minimal effort into your little one.

4. Your Child's Speech Is Inconsistent

Incoherent speech is the most common in very young toddlers. They may invent new terms to express themselves. The same word may be uttered differently throughout their speech, resulting in inconsistent pronunciation. For instance, your child may want to say "goodbye," but instead says "tie," "pie," or "die."

These might be symptoms of apraxia of speech in children (CAS). Early speech treatment, which you can have at home easily, may help lessen the persistence of the signs and symptoms later in life.

5. Your Child's Voice Is Unrecognizable

Perhaps you've noticed your child's voice has become abnormally raspy or harsh. Your child may also have difficulty managing their vocal level. Every toddler can get a sore throat and a hoarse voice from time to time. It's typical after loudly applauding during a baseball game or drinking too many ice Slurpees.

Chronic dysphonia may necessitate speech therapy which you can easily employ at home to restore correct vocal cord function.

6. Your Baby Is Making Phonological Errors

Is your three-year-old still using the word "fun" instead of "thumb"? Is "ba-wa-wa" being used instead of "ba-na-na"?

It is critical to have them indulge in activities that help your child develop better speech in these situations. These symptoms might indicate that your child's articulatory muscles are weak or having problems synchronizing the action of their speech muscles.

7. Your Child Doesn't Make Any Gestures Or Points

Your kid should be pointing at items and waving to people by their first birthday. But, of course, some kids make more minor gestures than others. If your kid makes no gestures, you should first consult your physician.

It can be a precursor to autism spectrum disorder (ASD). However, when begun early, speech therapy for autism can considerably aid a child's speech and language abilities.

8. Difficulty Understanding Your Kid's Speech

Any stranger should be able to comprehend a child's speech 50% of the time by two. However, if your toddler's vocabulary isn't clear enough, you can consult a speech therapist. The speech therapist can assist you in obtaining an accurate diagnosis and ask you to do home base speech therapies.

9. Kid With Cleft Palate

This common congenital disability can make it hard for your child to speak. If your kid has a cleft lip and palate, you should see your pediatrician as soon as possible. Surgery can fix a cleft palate and restore standard articulatory capabilities in a kid in various situations.

Home-based speech therapy may be required for an older kid to learn or re-learn how to generate accurate sounds when speaking.

10. Is Your Child Born With Down's Syndrome?

It gets hard sometimes to understand your child, which is heartbreaking! But speech therapy can help you out. Down's syndrome speech therapy can assist your kid in developing the required speech and language abilities.

You can help your kid learn to speak correctly and improve their overall communication abilities.

11. Child With Cerebral Palsy (CP)

Many children with cerebral palsy can not only learn to talk virtually clearly with continued speech therapy at home, but they can also learn to chew and swallow securely.

Alternative and augmentative communication (AAC) strategies such as using imageboards can be taught to your kid during speech treatment for cerebral palsy.

12. Your Child Isn't Interacting With Others At School

When your child is at home, they speak and express their opinions freely, but when they are at school or on the playground, they do not.

If a kid has selective mutism, it is typical for teachers and caregivers to complain about their child's lack of communication. It's a severe anxiety problem that prevents kids from speaking in public. Historically, it hasn't been classified as a speech-language disorder. However, with the support of parents and a speech therapist, your child may overcome their nervousness.

Will My Child's Speech Problems Be Overcome?

They say "thoup" rather than "soup." Is this an indication that they have a speech disorder? Are they going to require speech therapy? Will they be able to grow out of it on their own?

These are the few most commonly asked questions by concerned parents.

Although there are no clinical tests to identify whether your kid is a late talker or has an actual speech impairment, a comprehensive speech examination is the most conclusive answer to whether your child will ever outgrow his speech issues.

How much time does it take for your kid to recover from a speech disorder?

The time it takes for a patient to recover after therapy varies depending on their disease and the treatment style. The severity of their condition determines the capacity of people with persistent impairments to heal. More than one 4- to 8-week therapy session might result in some positive results.

Three Factors Determine If A Speech Challenge Will Be Overcome

To decide whether to proceed with therapy, the parents and speech therapists must carefully consider each issue, commonly done in conjunction with a speech screening or comprehensive assessment.

1. Severity Factor

Let's pretend that a misarticulated /r/ is the only sound your kid has trouble with. If the kid is still in kindergarten or below, you should usually take a "wait and see" approach. However, if self-correction does not occur after six months, you should be more inclined to visit a speech therapist and start home-based therapy. Likewise, if that same kindergartener had trouble with /s/ and /ch/ in addition to /r/, you should be inclined to start treatment right away.

2. Age Factor

From a motoric, movement-based approach, speech is the most sophisticated thing that humans perform daily. As a result, it's not unexpected that developing correct, fluent speech takes time for the average youngster. "How old is your child?" is probably the first thing that each parent should consider. Certain mispronunciations are relatively common. For example, it is common for a three-year-old to pronounce "wock" instead of "rock." However, determining the child's age is a delicate balancing act. Early intervention, according to research, is critical. However, you would not want to meddle if the kid corrected his mistakes on his own.

3. Family History

Another factor to examine when determining the severity of a kid's misarticulations is if the child has a history of speech problems and speech treatment and whether speech faults run in the family. For example, if your kid at the age of three speaks misarticulated /k, g, v, f/, it is much more probable that a misarticulated /s/ or /r/ will require therapy at the age of five. In addition, there is a substantial hereditary link to speech difficulties.

A comprehensive speech examination by a professional SLP is the most conclusive answer to whether a child will outgrow his speech issues. Age, intensity, and a child's or family's history of speech difficulties all play a role in concluding whether to intervene at a particular stage.

Let's do a short activity for kids to improve speech:

Name _____   Date _____

TURKEY PARTS

Cut out the words in the boxes below, then paste the words in the boxes.

| wattle | tail | wing | claw |
| beak | snood | feather | body |

Name _____ Date _____

TURKEY PARTS

Write the parts of a turkey into each box, then write a short paragraph to describe a turkey.

Write a short paragraph to describe all the parts of a turkey.

_____
_____
_____

TURKEY PARTS

A turkey is a type of bird that lives on a farm. Some families eat turkeys on Thanksgiving.

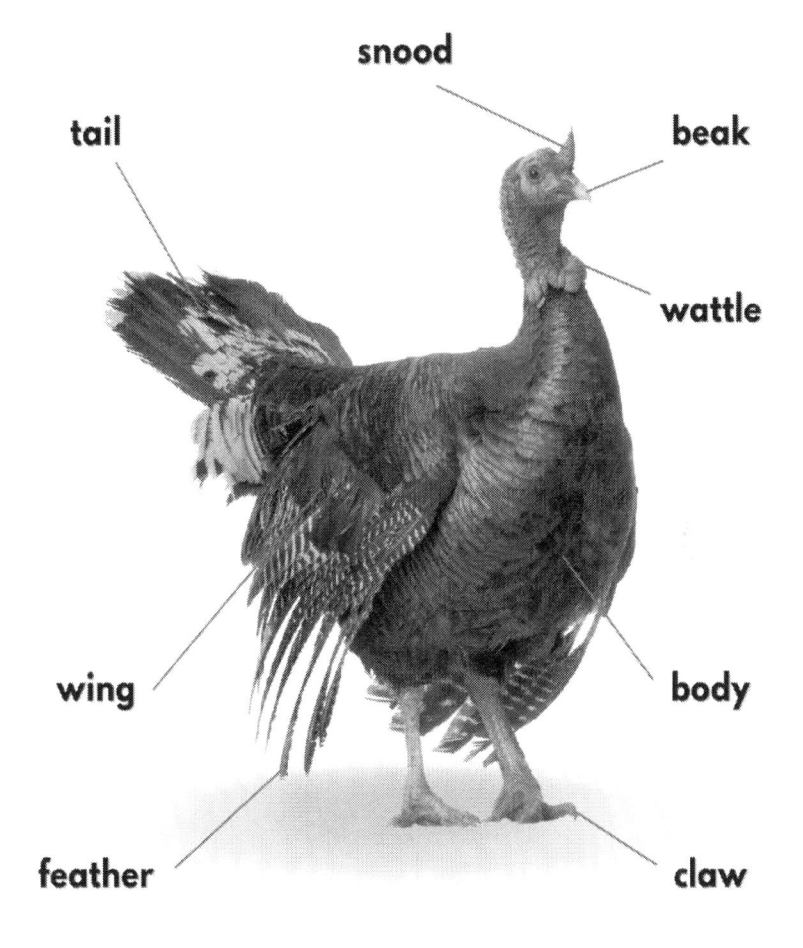

- snood
- tail
- beak
- wattle
- wing
- body
- feather
- claw

Time For Parents To Help Their Children, More Power To You All

Different Strategies For Speech Therapy That Parents Can Employ At Home

The work of a speech-language pathologist does not cease when the speech therapy session is completed. One of the most crucial components of their job is training parents and caregivers to elicit speech and language from their children at home.

In modern society, speech therapy does not last 30-60 minutes per week; these essential skills are performed weekly. Yet, that's how kids learn best, make the most significant progress toward their objectives, and apply new abilities in their everyday lives.

Here are different ways that anyone with a kid having a speech disorder may do at home.

Play Using Commands

According to researchers, 36.4% of children who left an early intervention program did not learn this ability. You may assist as a parent. You can also use [Story Cues Skilled Sequencing Cards](#).

For a child with impaired speech, playtime is an excellent educational opportunity. While it may be challenging to persuade your child to sit quietly and motionless at a desk, they may enjoy working with you on swings, yard, or in a pool.

Look for methods to convince your youngster to take control of the game's rules. Pose questions like:

- How should we proceed?"
- Will it be my turn?"
- Should we take a risk and leap or run?"

If your kid isn't reacting, model your responses. "What should we do next?" is an example of a phrase you may use. "Tell me, 'We're going to sprint,' or 'We're going to leap.'" If necessary, continue until your kid chooses an option and tells you about it.

Get In Some Name Recognition Practice

Many children with disorders do not turn their heads or respond when their names are uttered. It's a symptom of the illness.

Motivational training, according to experts, can help you develop this talent at home. **To do so, follow these steps:**

- First, approach your kid when they are occupied.
- Then, say your child's name ten times.
- Finally, give a mild shoulder touch while repeating your child's name if they don't answer.
- If your child still doesn't reply, gently move their head in your direction while pronouncing their name with your hands.
- Give a verbal incentive at the first evidence of a reaction, even if you must prod it. "Nice job listening to your name!" you may remark.

Repetition is critical, and after your kid has mastered the game, make it more difficult. While mentioning your name, gesture to yourself with your finger. Then ask, "What is your name?" pointing to your kid. If necessary, provide an immediate response.

Play The Game "I Spy."

While this may not be appropriate for all children with autism, even a few minutes on the patio can provide your kid with new experiences.

All objects you observe, including automobiles, plants, insects, and animals, should be pointed out and named. If your kid is paying attention, you can narrate. Then add 'I Spy' to the mix.

- "Do you see anything enormous and green?"
- "What exactly is it?"
- "Did you see anything little and wet?"
- "Can you tell me where it is?"
- "Do you see something broad and brown?".
- "Can you tell me where it is?"

Praise your kid for answers to any question; even if the response is nonverbal, keep the questions coming. For instance, if your child points, ask, "What is it called?" Moreover, you can also use Quick Card Game.

Emotions Should Be Labeled

Children's emotional literacy abilities may not always come readily. However, they are educated by parents and instructors who are gentle with them. These skills can help toddlers avoid tantrums and emotional outbursts and grow into caring individuals who know what others want and need. You can also play with Emotional Intelligence Flashcard Game.

For those with autism, emotional literacy is very crucial. They frequently have difficulty interpreting body language, particularly facial emotions. They may wish to comprehend what others desire, becoming irritated when their interpretations appear incorrect.

Collaborate with your child to develop these abilities.

- **Discuss Different Emotions**

Tell your toddler when you're pleased, delighted, furious, or sad. Simple sentences like "I'm sad" or "I'm incredibly pleased" would suffice. Make sure your kid can see your face and body position at that precise time.

- **Talk About Your Child's Feelings**

"Are you upset?" ask your kid if you notice a frown. "You seem incredibly pleased right now," mention if you observe a wide smile. Encourage your youngster to respond to your questions with phrases like "Yes, I am glad."

- **Make Use Of Media Prompts**

Actors and actresses display a great deal of emotion. Inquire about the feelings of the characters with your kid. Other media prompts like <u>Language Flash Card Library</u> are also efficient.

It's not the time to define feelings and speak through them if your kid is throwing a tantrum. Instead, look for opportunities to talk about your emotions before they get out of hand.

- **Read As A Group**

When they attend kindergarten, children with reading parents have heard nearly a million more words than children without reading parents. This word gap severely restricts the vocabulary of youngsters whose parents do not read to them.

Stick to novels that are brief and colorful. Read slowly and calmly, pointing to each word as you go. If the terms refer to a visual on the website, mean to and name the elements inside the graphic. Some autistic kids like the soothing rhythm of reading and will stay focused and engaged for as long as they want to read. Others become agitated after one or two pages.

Soothe your child's agitation by promising a reward at the end of the session. Short sessions are good, as long as they are repeated frequently. If reading appears to be a stressful activity for your child, don't force them to do it. If your youngster isn't interested in reading, try the next day again. If they still refuse to read, wait a week before trying again.

- **Sing Songs With Your Youngster**

Some children with autism, according to experts, have a strong recall for song lyrics and television jingles. So put your rote memory to good use in your home speech treatment sessions. Request that your kid sing along to a favorite song. Stop your kid and ask a question about a lyric. To aid your learning, have your kid say the words to the musical.

Make use of <u>Speech Sounds Series like Gary the Goat</u>. Singing can also help your little one learn to control their voice's tempo and loudness. Encourage your youngster to sing quietly throughout the song's gentle passages, then open wide and sing loudly at the end.

- **Tell A Story About Your Day**

Your little one may be willing to assist in setting the table for supper, or you and your child might water plants together. Maintain a polite conversation regardless of what you're doing.

- Names.
- Verbs.
- Sequences.

From time to time, solicit your child's opinion. For example, "What is this?" you could ask as you hold out an object. "What happens next?" asks a person in the middle of an action.

- **Get Help Through Visuals**

For a toddler, everything is new. Parents must help their children's language learning while they're gaining new abilities at a quick pace. Let's look at how to utilize visuals as a tool in the parenting toolkit.

Some kids struggle to comprehend the different changes and routines that occur during the day. Putting illustrations of everyday routines on a bulletin board or in a book might help your little one anticipate what their day will be like and reduce any potential responses. They may even help decide what activities they'll do by choosing a play activity after snack and putting it on the board.

Spending time pointing out and labeling people in photographs can inspire your kid to do the same. You may use <u>Talking Flash Cards Speech Therapy Toys</u> as well.

A kitchen timer is another valuable visual aid that many people already have. These might make it easier for your youngster to adapt to everyday shifts or routines. For example, if getting your child dressed and out the door is a daily struggle, set a timer to signal when to clean up and leave home. This can be a helpful reminder!

- **Positive Reinforcement**

It's simple to say "don't do that" or "no" to a child. But, it's frequently an issue of personal safety.

At the same time, children must understand they've accomplished something beneficial.

We can get into the habit of saying "excellent work." But what exactly did you do well? "Wow, you ate all of your vegetables!" or "I adore how you have organized your toys all by yourself!" That's incredible!" It's critical to be detailed and point out exactly what your kid excelled in.

After all, positive reinforcement is something we all like and respond to.

- **Contingency Plans**

Many children find it challenging to follow instructions. Few things in life may be as aggravating as being a parent.

The contingency strategy may be helpful in several situations. Making a task that your child "wants" to complete dependent on a job that they "need" to accomplish is what this implies. For example, "After you finish eating your veggies, you can go outdoors and play."

This incentive system encourages your kid to follow directions so that everyone gets what they want!

- **Remove All Sources Of Distraction**

Play-based activities help young toddlers acquire language. When playing with your child, it's critical to get all potential distractions out of the way so that the training and real bonding time can happen. This is also true for parents! It includes shutting off the television, putting your phone away, and concealing other sources of stimulation.

- **Laugh At Yourself**

Strange sounds, goofy looks, and exaggerated speech elicit a response from children. Make animal sounds or automobile beeps to get down on their level. Make goofy expressions in the bathtub with a mirror. Give your kid a burst of energy during playtime to let them know it's alright to play around with their voice.

They'll be more interested and willing to contribute if you're silly.

Start doing all of these things at home right now! You may assume that this is sufficient to restore your child's linguistic abilities to normal levels.

Let's do an activity for kids to improve speech:

BODY PARTS

The outside of the human body has many different parts that work together.

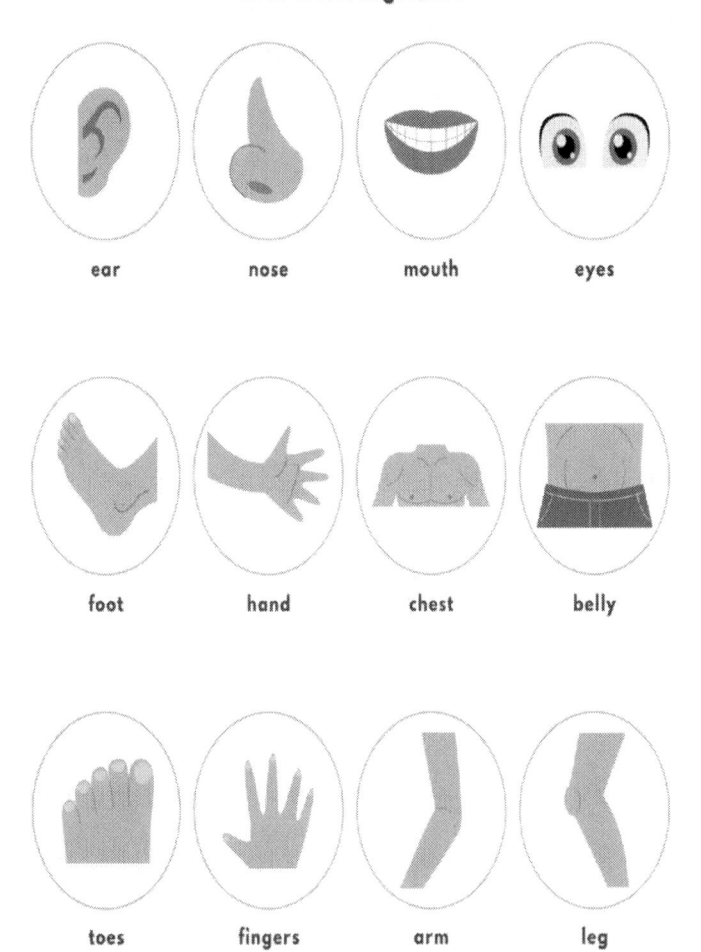

ear	nose	mouth	eyes
foot	hand	chest	belly
toes	fingers	arm	leg

WHEN QUESTIONS

When do you go swimming?
In the summer

When do you sleep?
At night

When do you drink water?
When you're thirsty

When do you wear a costume?
On Halloween

When questions ask about a time or moment

When do you eat food?
When you're hungry

When do you take a bath?
When you're dirty

When do flowers grow?
In the spring

Make Homeschooling For Children With Autism Enjoyable And Effective

Because of the abrupt and rapid spread of COVID-19, many institutions and companies have been forced to shut down. In addition, due to the closure of many speech therapy clinics, many people are left at home with their children, confused about keeping the structure and learning a part of their child's day. This approach will provide you with a fair notion of how to continue in the weeks ahead (and perhaps months).

The essential things are to develop a daily schedule for your child, have a range of entertaining activities on hand, and maintain your sanity throughout this extraordinary period.

Homeschooling a kid with autism is a challenging and unique endeavor, but it can be accomplished by planning and adapting the following strategies.

Assist Them In Making Connections With Reality

This may be accomplished by linking their passions with real-life things or circumstances. Your kid, for example, is fascinated with space exploration. Bring him to a planetarium or give him a telescope to play with so he can learn about the actual world.

Supporting his enthusiasm will motivate him to study, speak about it and keep his attention.

Take Advantage Of Fixations
Children with autism spectrum conditions are prone to get obsessed with themes. This single-mindedness, on the other hand, can be advantageous. Incorporate whatever your kid is now obsessed with into your teaching! This will help children recall the knowledge as they study, keeping their attention and making the learning process entertaining.

Take Breaks In Your Sessions
Working nonstop for lengthy periods can be overwhelming for any kid, especially with autism. This may be one of the reasons why particular kids struggle in regular schooling. So, if you're homeschooling your child, don't make them work long hours.

Take breaks throughout the day instead. The most trouble-free way to achieve this is to enable your kid to relax and concentrate by taking brief pauses between lessons. If you don't do this, your child may get too exhausted by the end of the day to fully absorb the knowledge you're giving them.

Socialization In The Real World

Many parents are concerned about how their children with autism will interact with others in real-life circumstances. This is crucial when your child is removed from public school and spends less time with other kids.

You may still socialize with your kid by taking them on regular walks. You may re-center these field excursions around your child's obsessions to keep them interested and involved.

Maintain A Schedule

Maintaining a schedule is one strategy to assist your child is staying on track. When children with speech disorders have some order in their day, they perform very well. However, if you switch up your schedule every day, your child can have problems focusing on work or transferring from one job to another.

It's also a good idea to post this schedule somewhere where your child can see it every day and refer to it during the day. You may make this schedule colorful and interactive if you wish so that your child can "mark off" items they do during the day.

Avoid Quackery Treatments
Parents! Here's the deal. There is no fast fix, oil, diet, supplement, or detox program that can assist your youngster in speaking. When your child's brain learns to process language, they will talk. But unfortunately, some of them are a complete waste of time and money, while others are detrimental to your child's growth.

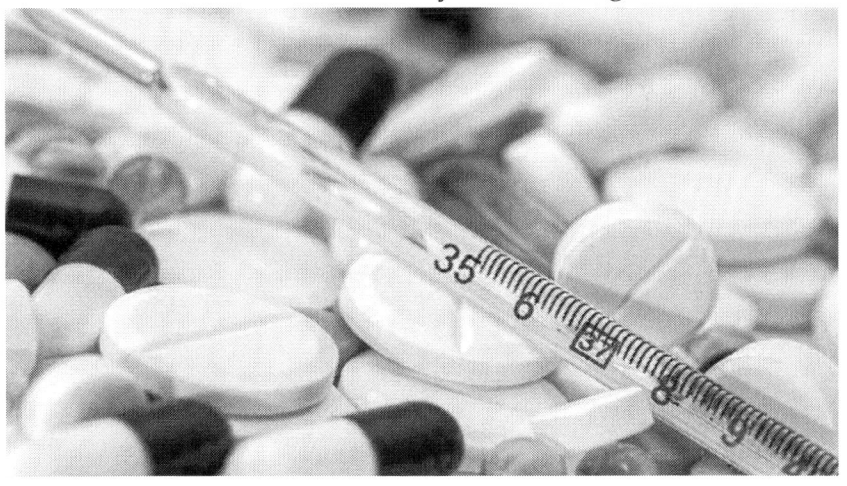

Include Activities and Subjects Which Motivate Them To Learn

Consider how challenging everything is for a child with language and speech impairment. Because everything they do is reliant on language, it is a battle, and they are frequently surrounded by others who do not share their challenges, their self-worth suffers greatly.

Finding hobbies and subjects in which they thrive is highly motivating since it gives them a sense of success.

- If your child is fascinated by trucks, use this interest to retain concentration and attention. Rather than being concerned that these obsessions may distract your child, you can exploit them. In addition, including exciting topics in your daily lessons will encourage kids to speak out and engage.

- When you observe your child struggling and becoming frustrated in a subject, you will cut that subject short and shift him to a topic you know he enjoys and is exceptionally excellent at. It's astonishing how quickly he returns to the prior subject and can finish the assignment with no difficulty because his sense of accomplishment is boosted!

Give Them Time And Chances
Time is the best friend of a child with speech and language disorder. Allow time for their brain to grow, comprehend what you're saying, and form their phrases.

Make A Few Movements
Another struggle for a child with Autism is sitting still for long periods. We've previously discussed how you can break up this by taking breaks from your lesson plans, yet you can do one more thing: include movement in your lecture. Rather than reading from a textbook or taking notes, consider an activity where you and your child may run about, bounce around, and have fun while learning.

Please Take It Slow
Don't become overly enthusiastic when you're ready to homeschool your child. If you buy a lot of textbooks and supplies, you're probably not going to use them all. Instead, spend a few weeks observing how your child learns and works best. You may modify your lesson plans to match your child's requirements once you know how and where they perform best.

Here's what people should know about your child while speaking with them:
• Your child is not delayed in development. However, they have a linguistic barrier.

- Your child can speak; you need to give them time.
- Your child does not require you to finish their sentences for them. Allow them to speak and be heard.

Finally, Don't Believe You're On Your Own
Homeschooling an autistic kid is a significant undertaking, but several tools are available, ranging from internet materials and services to professional assistance such as authorized learning partners.

SEEK ASSISTANCE
Suppose there's one thing you can be grateful for on this journey. In that case, it's the support you can have received from other parents who have traveled this path before or who are currently doing so and who can remind you to enjoy the journey and resist the temptation to scrutinize every move your child makes out of fear.

You'll need the help of others to remind you that you're not alone, to push back against the worry and anxiety, and to appreciate your children right now, today. Not when they evolve in a more usual manner. Not when they're on the same level as their classmates. Now is the right time.

22 Things To Help Your Children With Speech Disorders Gain Confidence

If your young kid has a speech disability, you're probably looking for assistance to help them cope as they become older. When children's speech is affected, it's easy to understand how they might develop emotional and psychological disorders due to a loss of self-esteem. Confidence is critical to a child's happiness, health, and success in the future. Confident children can better handle peer pressure, responsibilities, disappointments, obstacles, and sound and negative emotions.

Difficulty in speech and language can lead to emotional, behavioral, and psychological issues. They've linked the behavior to terror and dread. They have the right to be concerned; they face a significant danger of being harassed at school.

Do you know the most crucial factor in developing a child's confidence?

YOU! Parents

Isn't there any pressure? You can even make it enjoyable!

Start improving your children's confidence with these 22 research-based, practical tactics.

1. **Make Them Believe That Your Love Is Unconditional**

How we view our children significantly influences how they see themselves. You should make sure that they know how much you love them and are there for them.

2. **Call Them By Their First Name**

When combined with polite eye contact, addressing children by name is a solid and straightforward approach to communicating the message that they are valuable.

3. Assign Age-Appropriate "Special Responsibilities" To Children To Assist You

Give children "special projects" in addition to housework and classroom assignments to make them feel valuable, responsible, and capable. Using the adjective "special" boosts children's self-esteem even more.

These chores at home might involve assisting with a pet or younger sibling, acting as your kitchen "helper," or just dressing oneself for a tiny child.

4. Participate In Their Game (And Let Them Lead)

Participating in a child's play conveys that he is valuable and deserving of your attention. Parents can enable children to begin or pick the activity during playtime and lead it. The child feels practical and successful when parents participate in and enjoy a child-led activity.

5. Work On Boosting Your Self-Assurance

This isn't something you can do in a day, but it's one of the most critical steps on the list. Because parents are their children's first and most significant role models, take the time to rebuild your self-esteem if necessary. Begin by making good remarks about yourself and others in front of your child.

6. Seek Their Advice Or Point Of View

To demonstrate that you appreciate children and their thoughts, ask them for their advice or comments on age-appropriate circumstances. This also helps kids gain confidence by showing that even adults require assistance from time to time and that it is OK to ask for it.

7. Spend Quality Time Together

Take him on trips, have supper with him, play games with him, walk outside, or do anything else that will allow you and your child to spend quality time together. Parents also may make kids feel liked and welcomed by learning about their interests or hobbies and conducting tailored interactions with each child, such as "How was your soccer game yesterday, Sarah?" or "I think you would like this dinosaur book, Timmy?"

8. Instruct Them On How To Create And Attain Objectives

Children can feel more capable by setting and attaining challenging, realistic objectives. Assist your children or pupils in setting and achieving goals.

9. Make Time To Offer Them Your Complete Attention

Your kid can tell if you're thinking about anything else or not giving him your full attention. Therefore, you may devote your complete focus to kids and pay close attention to their requirements.

10. Persuade Them To Enroll In A Drama Class

Theater courses are a fantastic method to increase your self-esteem. Trying new things makes kids feel capable, and theater encourages them to speak boldly in front of people and step outside their comfort zone. Parents and teachers may both encourage their children to visit a theater, and instructors can even introduce role-playing or drama activities into the classroom.

11. Give Them Appropriate Praise

While showing children praise is ineffective, appropriately praising them can help them develop self-esteem. Give honest, personalized credit to kids that emphasize effort rather than outcomes (such as straight A's) or fixed skills (like intelligence).

12. Don't Make Comparisons To Others

Avoid queries like "Why can't you act like him/her?" or "Look how wonderfully your sister succeeds in school!" that compare kids to siblings or peers. Instead, "Why aren't you able to accomplish that?"

These comparisons encourage kids to question themselves, believing that they will never be able to please you or reach your expectations, and eventually lose faith in themselves.

13. Assign Age-Appropriate Responsibilities Around The House

When children perform chores or minor tasks, they feel they are contributing something useful, which gives them a sense of competence and confidence.

14. Encourage Them To Feel Like They Belong By Displaying Their Photographs Or Artwork Throughout The House

Yes, even simple things like displaying family photographs about the house may boost your child's self-esteem! You may also submit images of your kids in the classroom. You might also have students do self-portraits, design flags or puzzle pieces that symbolize their personalities and hobbies, and then display them throughout the school.

This provides kids a sense of belonging, acceptance, and affection, boosting their self-esteem.

15. Allow Them To Make Decisions Based On Their Age

Like chores and special assignments, choices provide youngsters with a sense of competence and authority. Allow children to make decisions like; what to dress, what to eat for breakfast, what game or color to play, where to travel on a trip, etc.

16. Encourage Them To Attempt New Things

Children with low self-esteem are typically hesitant to try new things or take on new tasks. Encourage your children to attempt new things, try new hobbies, and learn new abilities.

17. Help Them With Their Hobbies

It's also critical for children to identify their hobbies and passions. Children build confidence in themselves and their talents when they discover what they enjoy and succeed at. So create chances for your children to participate in things they are interested in, and encourage them to do so.

18. Assist Them In Overcoming Their Fear Of Failing

Children's fear of failure frequently inhibits them from giving it their all and attaining their full potential, leading to a loss of confidence. Help children overcome their fear of failure by educating them that making errors is an inevitable part of life and that success is rarely achieved without obstacles and setbacks. Please encourage them to express their emotions by giving them opportunities. When you criticize or dismiss a child's sentiments, he may assume that his feelings are unimportant. Encourage kids to express both happy and negative emotions and assist them in healthily talking about them.

19. Make It Clear That You're Disappointed In Their Decisions, Not In Who They Are

Naturally, you'll sometimes be frustrated with your children, and you'll need to deliver constructive criticism and penalties. Make it evident that you're dissatisfied with the child's choices or actions, not with who the kid is as a person. Instead of scolding the youngster with remarks like "You're so sloppy!" or "Why are you so sloppy?" direct all criticism towards their acts.

20. Surround Them With Upbeat And Confident Individuals (Including Their Friends)

The more positive, confident people a youngster is exposed to, the more likely he will grow convinced and optimistic. So, teachers, provide a good and confident example for your children by teaching them to be friendly and build each other up.

21. Celebrate Their Accomplishments By Erecting A Wall Of Fame

A Wall of Fame may recognize a child's hard work and perseverance, providing him with confidence that can be especially beneficial during moments of self-doubt.

22. Give them lots of hugs!

Physical affection conveys love, acceptance, and belonging to kids, helping them feel secure and joyful.

Make Your Autistic Kid A Fluent Speaker

A kid with autism may be unable to communicate for various reasons. The primary way to tell if your kid has nonverbal autism is by keeping a check on their speech pattern.

Let's have a look at why this could be happening. As the disorder's symptoms increase, autistic kids may lose their communication capacity. This may prevent the child from saying what they wish to express. This might also make it challenging to communicate clearly.

Nonverbal autism also manifests social, behavioral, and developmental characteristics.

When a two-year-old autistic child's name is called, they may not answer. A nonverbal autistic four-year-old may repeat meaningless words and phrases. A nonverbal autistic five-year-old may have difficulty comprehending gestures in a communicative situation.

Do Non-Verbal Autistic Toddlers Babble?
Around 40% of autistic children are unable to communicate. However, others may talk despite their weak language and communication abilities. Babbling happens when a baby is learning to speak. They move their tongues in various ways and open and close their mouths. Babies who are generally developing chatter to begin their early language development.
Suppose a nonverbal youngster with autism babbles while maintaining eye contact or making gestures toward others.
Help your autistic kid to talk.
One strategy that works for one kid may not work for another. However, with the support of treatments and

assistance, nonverbal autistic people can have and live entire and comfortable lives.

- **Medicine:** There is no unique drug that can heal autism. Anxiety or sadness in a kid is possible, and medication might help.
- **Counseling:** Counseling parents, caregivers, and siblings of people with autism might be pretty beneficial. They can learn how to handle the problem to obtain favorable outcomes and manage the obstacles of nonverbal autism through therapy.
- **Structured sessions are highly beneficial to children with autism:** They can improve their social and linguistic skills while receiving an education and focusing on personal growth.

What Is In The Future Of Your Kid?

It is critical that, with the correct assistance, kids can acquire the required skills to live everyday life.

Children with autism communicate in various ways, even though they are nonverbal.

Being unable to communicate should not be viewed as a setback but rather as a task that may be met. Although there is no magic cure for speech, your kid may be able to make significant progress with your help. They will have a more favorable attitude about communication once they comprehend and acquire a technique to convey what they are experiencing, whether verbal or nonverbal.

When Will My Autistic Child Start Talking?
Language milestones are typically delayed in autistic children with verbal communication than in children with typical development.

While ordinarily developing baby create their first words between the ages of 12 and 18 months, autistic children do it at 36 months on average. Because each autistic child's development is unique, the period at which they generate their first words varies.

Until recently, parents and caregivers of autistic children were led to think that if their kids did not talk by the age of 4 or 5, they would never speak again.

How To Communicate With A Non-Verbal Autistic Child

You can assist your nonverbal autistic child in communicating in so many ways. They don't take the place of speech therapy or other therapies tailored to your child's specific requirements. However, they may be a big help at home in establishing contact with your child.

Use Straightforward Language

Avoid utilizing sentences with many words. Instead, use one or two-word statements wherever possible. This will assist them in improving without becoming overburdened.

Consider Various Options

Nonverbal children with autism may express their feelings with dancing, painting, or hand and body movements. You might attempt finger painting or sensory exercises to help kids express themselves better.

Seek Help From Technology

As further mentioned in our guide, various programs and gadgets are available to assist with technology.

Let Them Observe You

Sit in front of your kid, at eye level. This places you in their line of sight, allowing them to observe your emotions, facial expressions, and lip movements. This way, they'll be able to read your body language and understand what you're saying.

How To Keep Your Child Committed To Meet His Speech Standards?

The more you can assist your kids in using methods acquired in live therapy at home, the faster they'll be able to achieve their communication objectives.

But we support you that this is not at all easy.

The short solution is to maintain a pleasant attitude while practicing. The exciting and enjoyable practice makes your kid engage more freely than resist.

This guide will give you helpful suggestions for your child to meet his speech goals and standards with at-home speech therapy as the most enjoyable part of your child's day!

Choose The Appropriate Level Of Complexity

Part of the reason children struggle to participate in speaking exercises is because they might be difficult. When kids have difficulty, they might grow discouraged and unmotivated to practice. While the communication goals being pursued may appear easy to you and me, they may be overwhelming to your youngster.

If you feel that your kid is becoming frustrated, try the following:

- o Reduce the assignment's difficulty level
- o Provide additional cueing to assist your kid in completing the task

Another advantage is your youngster's great feeling after accomplishing a goal. Giving them some small activities will help your kid feel accomplished. In addition, they will be much more inclined to take on more demanding activities once their confidence in their ability to finish a spoken assignment develops!

Maintain A Healthy Practice Frequency

It's critical to strike a "sweet spot" regarding how often you and your youngster practice.

"Should I tell my child if I notice a mispronunciation or something they say improperly?" many parents may question. Much to the amazement of many parents, our response is "No." Allow me to explain.

What if someone was continually correcting what you said throughout the day? Is that something that would discourage you? Definitely Yes!

Would that make you want to practice with that individual less? Yes, of course!

Your kid is in the same boat.

A reasonable rule of thumb is to practice 20-30 minutes per day, 5-7 days per week. You are the most excellent judge of your child's attention span, so choose the perfect practice time for them!

You may also model the speech objectives for your child outside of these planned practice hours. In this manner, your kid sees and hears you speaking the correct pronunciation regularly, without feeling obligated to practice all day.

Consider the following scenario: your kid is working on creating their /s/ sound. You may demonstrate proper /s/ production for your child throughout the day by pointing out different words and things in your surroundings that begin with the /s/ sound.

This type of speech model, along with the disciplined practice, is the ideal combination to assist your child in achieving their goals.

Encourage And Congratulate Them

This significant area of learning is the one that we are pretty passionate about. Always remember to praise your child no matter how your practice goes with them or how many chores they get correctly or wrong!

It might be challenging to do this since it is still necessary to call out wrong replies. Children can only progress by being aware of correct and incorrect answers. However, strike a careful balance by including some favorable remarks.

Here are a few of my favorite things to say to a kid who is having difficulty with a task:

- ✓ " I'm impressed with how hard you're working!
- ✓ Maybe that's not it, but I can see you're working hard.!"
- ✓ "You're a fighter who never gives up!" Let us continue to improve our abilities. I'm confident you'll be able to do it!"

And, of course, let your child know when they're doing very well with their speech objectives.

Rewarding children for working towards completing an activity may be quite effective. Make sure that your youngster knows how much work they must complete for receiving the reward. Please give them a set length of time to do the task in exchange for the prize. Anything may be used as a reward. Here are a few suggestions:

1. Videos

2. Music (play a song, a section of a song, or sing it)

3. Puzzle pieces (one at a time)

4. Sticker charts

5. Games (basketball, iPad, Candyland, etc.)

Points for good work must be won in small increments to keep the therapy session focused on the task at hand. Giving kids a choice between prizes appeals to some. However, it can be beneficial to provide them with options before they start working to feel more in control of the situation.

Note: Offering food as a reward is not recommended.

Time To Roll, Parents! The Most Interesting Part Is Here. Speech Therapy Activities At Home

Activities And Games To Aid At Home Speech Therapy

Speech therapists employ a variety of engaging activities to assist their clients in practicing language production, ranging from word games to board games and beyond. As a layman, you may try out the same exercises with your loved one at home.

Pre-Schoolers Speech Therapy Games

These engaging preschool games are ideal language activities for children of all ages.

1. **Word Play Hopscotch**

Draw hopscotch and write target words in each box on the sidewalk or driveway. Then, as they progress through the game, have the player pronounce the words aloud to develop speech sounds.

It aids in pronunciation.

2. I Spy

One player selects an object in the room that all players can see and then hints to the other players to guess what they are thinking about. The player who correctly guesses the word must use it in a sentence.

Assists with Turn-taking, sentence fluency

3. The Alphabet Game

The Alphabet Game is the most fun hack to learn the alphabet.

Have the player look for all the alphabet letters on signs while driving or strolling about your area. Older players can use a piece of paper to write down each letter they locate. Then, make them utter a word that begins with each letter they find as an extra challenge.

It aids in pronunciation.

4. Find A Word

There are many different difficulty levels for word searches, so find one appropriate for the player's age. Then, have them repeat the word loudly when they locate it. It's suitable for children aged 5 to 7.

It aids in pronunciation.

5. Word-Based Hide-And-Seek

Request that the player locates word cards that you have placed about the home. Let them say aloud the word on the card when they discover it. Use image cards for individuals who can't read.

Assists with Pronunciation

6. App For Articulation Station

Little Bee Speech's Articulation Station app is for children aged 4 and up. The program includes stages of practice for words, sentences, and stories.

Word discovery, phrase fluency, and pronunciation are all aided by this program.

School Going Speech Therapy Games

1. Speech And Yoga Therapy

When you combine speech therapy with yoga, you may have double the enjoyment.

Word discovery, phrase fluency, and pronunciation are all aided by this program.

2. Contrary To Popular Belief, Opposites Attract.

One player creates a list of terms with an apparent opposite, such as "yes," "down," "glad," and so on. Then, one player reads each word while the other player says the opposite.

Word searching and speaking, in turn, are two things that it can help with.

3. Keep A Journal

Writing in a diary can help people improve their language output and comprehension since reading and language development are linked. First, provide the children with a set of writing prompts from which to pick. Then, allow them to register for 5 or 10 minutes without stopping.

It aids in word-finding and sentence fluency.

Children and adults can feel more confident and build their skills to speak successfully via speech therapy activities. Also, please peek at our other speech therapist resources.

8 Ways Of Technology To Help Home-Based Speech Therapy

Few professions have remained unaffected by fast technological innovation and transition. Unfortunately, speech disorders are no exception.

Historically, therapist-client interactions were more likely to be restricted and compartmentalized from parents and family members. While SLPs use their expertise and experience to treat the underlying speech and language difficulties, a lack of collaboration with stakeholders might easily result in overlooked treatment opportunities.

Many digital tools and new technology may improve speech therapy delivery. There are hundreds of apps and online tools that are free and can assist your child in improving their communication abilities with speech therapy at home if you have access to a mobile device such as an iPad.

Let's look at some of the latest breakthroughs in speech-language pathology and the implications for children, families, and speech therapists.

How To Use Speech Therapy Software Efficiently?

Everyone may use apps, but they are precious for children who need to fix or enhance their inadequacies.

A few apps can be quite beneficial to those with communication or cognitive difficulties.

Articulation Station

Why Choose This?

Your child's speech abilities will improve in no time, thanks to various exercises designed to help them practice words, phrases, and understanding. It helps with these features.

- Playback of voice recordings
- Progress notes and data logging

Slingo (For Toddlers)

Why Choose This?

Your child may create a fundamental grasp of language that will last a lifetime by beginning at level 1 and getting better on their way up to level 4.

- Kid-friendly outer space theme
- Difficulty levels rise as your child gets older.
- Improves listening and language learning abilities

Speech Tutor (Best For Elementary)

Why Choose This?

Animated videos at variable speeds let your child picture how sounds are produced in the mouth and back of the throat, making even the most difficult sounds easier to master.

Lamp Words For Life (The Most Suitable For Autism)

Why Choose This?

LAMP Words for Life focuses on building common patterns of speech and conversation for autistic children who struggle with verbal communication.

Proloquo2Go (Best For Non-Communicators)

Why Choose This?

Nonverbal kids can communicate again and, in some cases, recover their verbal communication skills — thanks to realistic text-to-speech technology. In addition, the organization's features make it simple to access and track progress.

Apraxia Therapy (Best For Apraxia)

Why Choose This?

This software combines audio, visual, and tactical techniques to help children with apraxia improve their communication abilities. You may work at three different speeds with the Apraxia Therapy app, allowing you to customize the curriculum to your kid's specific requirements. It also includes colloquial terms that you may encounter regularly. Then you may go back and listen to the tape to see how far your child has come.

- Multi-sensory approach with touch and audio learning
- Customizable practice words depending on your own needs
- History record for later review and correction

DAF Pro (Best For Stuttering)

Why Choose This?

Use recorded playback to let your kid learn changes in speech. An app may run in the background without consuming a kid's energy. Teaches your kid to slow down and speak more clearly

The Speech Tools DAF Pro software allows children who stutter or stammer to slow down their speech so that it is easier to understand others. While DAF Pro was created to help children with stuttering and stammering, it is also advised for neurological diseases like Parkinson's. Delayed Auditory Feedback, or DAF, is a speech and language treatment strategy designed to assist children who chatter learn to speak more slowly.

Social Apps Which Help Strengthen Social Bonds

Another issue that kids with speech and language problems or challenges encounter are social isolation. It is critical to maintaining contact with others to strengthen social communication abilities. Technology has simplified social interactions and relationships, and you may use it at home to assist your kid with communication difficulties.

Pinterest

Yes, even Pinterest contains instructive, motivating, and entertaining activities. Courtesy of PediaStaff, you'll discover "apps of the week," "sound articulation game ideas," and even a posting dedicated to playing an April Fool's joke on your SLP.

365 Days of Playing With Words

This site is dedicated to helping children improve their speech. It offers a "freebies" area with various free, practical, and fun activities and ideas for your children. Vocabulary, writing and reading principles, speech and sound development, and much more are all covered.

Smarty Ears' House Of Learning

This is a fun iPad app created by speech-language pathologists as a learning and entertainment tool. This software allows kids to practice linguistic skills such as prepositions and narrative telling.

Choosing An App For Communication Problems

There are certain apps designed expressly for those who have difficulty communicating. Depending on the precise speech and language challenges, you may pick applications that will benefit your kid and work with them at home, utilizing the apps to aid with the problem. In most cases, the therapist will recommend communication applications, but if this is not the case, you may do your research to find the best app for your child. First, however, you must select the appropriate one for your child's talents and abilities.

- Charitable, CommunicAide, and Talk's Photos are helpful for those with language disabilities.
- Text-based programs like Verbally and ClaroCom can be pretty useful for those who have stuttering.
- AlphaTopis can also aid individuals who like to write, while HandySpeech can help those who want to speak naturally.
- Tobii Dynavox Compass, TouchChat, and Predictable are several AAC apps that enable text, symbols, and scenarios.

WORDS TO REMEMBER:

Technology can't take the place of a committed parent or caregiver who incorporates skill-building into their child's daily routine. The great majority of a child's speech and language acquisition occurs outside of speech therapy sessions or via the use of an app — it happens by listening and engaging with individuals in their environment (during playtime, at the park, trips to the grocery store, etc.). Parents are the best people to know their children and have several opportunities to engage with them throughout their lives. These everyday situations will continue to be the best opportunities for children to practice and reinforce skills that will help them attain their developmental milestones and become competent communicators.

Developing Pretend Plays As Effective Speech Therapy Techniques

Pretend play, also known as symbolic play, is vital for various reasons.

1. Gaining a better knowledge of the functions of various items
2. Expanding one's inventiveness and flexibility of thought
3. Learning about and playing out real-life scenarios
4. Language development typically occurs in tandem with pretend play

First Stage

Pretending to play with actual items is the first stage. This demonstrates that a youngster comprehends the nature of things and what we do with them. Next, name something that you play with.

Second Stage

Encourage the kid to associate things with other people once they have learned how to use them. For example, assist the kid in brushing her hair while saying " Brush Brush Brush."

Third Stage

Encourage the kid to imitate ordinary tasks at home, such as sweeping, washing cups, cooking, and washing clothing, in the third stage.

Teach and promote pretend play using everyday household items such as a teddy bear, doll, bed, table, food, and blanket. Extend the space into brief sequences, such as brushing the doll's hair, washing her face, and bathing. Let them make a story about what she is doing "Time to take a shower" As the kid gains confidence, continue to prolong these sequences.

Fourth Stage

Playing in a bit of the world is the fourth stage.

Make the switch to small-world toys like dollhouses, garages, or farms so that play is more creative and less reliant on actual items.

Around this time, you may assist the kid, in the beginning, to use items metaphorically, assuming that they are another thing, such as a phone or a banana. Let them talk about what they have to while pretending to be someone. Most kids love copying their parents.

The Fifth And Final Stage

It promotes intricate symbolism and role-playing.

Make the transition to small toys of all kinds – dolls' home stuff, matchbox automobiles, play people, farm and zoo animals, soldiers, and so on – so that real-life events and tales may be played out.

Extend the child's tales by offering new concepts, such as your automobile colliding with his car, in which case you summon an ambulance and hand over the breakdown lorry to him.

Increase the amount of verbal conversation between the toys and the physical interaction; for example, when the police car comes, you act out the policeman questioning the driver about the accident.

Increase the imaginative component so that the focus shifts from reality to fantasy, such as dressing up games and role play as a police officer or transforming empty boxes into boats, automobiles, and houses.

Allow kids to express their feelings and emotions, explain events, ask questions, provide directions, and play out the actual world.

Playing Ideas For Your Little Ones

You can adopt different kinds of plays at home to help your kid's speech disorder.

Playing Physically

Physical activity aids in developing mobility and coordination and may boost their confidence which lets them talk freely with anyone. Let your kid make new friends and let them play independently. This is the best way to help him learn and build his confidence.

Here are some suggestions for physical activity:

- Take the kid to a park or an outdoor play area where they may enjoy the swings, slides, and climbing structures
- Play ball games with your youngster at a level they would appreciate

- Allow little toddlers to splash and kick in the bath or puddles
- Play games like hide-and-seek and chase
- To encourage walking, use push-along toys
- Young children can be bounced on their knees or lifted and rocked in their arms
- Visit a soft-play center or incorporate one into your surroundings

Cause And Effect Plays

The following activities help grow language development, play, and fine motor skills.

- Toys that you may pull and push along
- Give the kid squeezable and shakable toys
- Make a tower out of cups or blocks, then knock it down
- Play with push-button musical toys, such as shakers, drums, keyboards, and xylophones. Books with lift-the-flaps and books that produce noises are popular

React to the child's movements and sounds with a positive, familiar reaction, such as "uh oh!", "oh no," "wow," yay," "there you go!", etc.

Playing With Building Materials

Construction Play aids a child's ability to enhance hand-eye coordination and movement abilities, comprehend how components fit together, and practice memory.

It also provides a sense of achievement that leads to learning new words.

- Toys can be hidden under clothes or crates, or things might be buried in the sand.
- Change the contents of containers and bags
- Dens may be made with chairs and bedding
- Bricks may be used to build skyscrapers, bridges, and dwellings
- Make jigsaw puzzles. Simple inset puzzles are the simplest
- Shape sorters are fun to play with

Exploratory And Sensory Play

Children tend to learn about the world around them via sensory and exploratory play. Sensory exploration allows kids to provide language stimulation and helps in functional learning.

You might try the following activities to enhance sensory and exploratory play.

- Encourage your youngster to put an eatable thing in his mouth and let him taste it. Tell him it is "yummy."

- Assist the kid in banging, shaking, inspecting, dropping, and throwing things. Ask him if it is "Noisy"?
- Bring together a variety of textures for the kid to feel and explore, such as rough, smooth, spiky, and feathers.
- Give your kid squeezable and shakable toys. Say words like" Wobbly" and "Shaky."
- Bells, rattles, and musical toys can be used to explore sounds. Let him do humming along.
- Play with brightly colored, sparkling, and lit-up toys and things. Tell him to repeat words like "wow" or "so shiny" after you.

People Play And Play Games

Children's eyes and ears are drawn to faces and voices, and they are considerably more interested in you than in a toy. People's games are activities that do not require toys and include you and your kid in a simple, calm atmosphere where you can both enjoy each other's company.

Tickles, quiet repeated voices with varying pitch, and physical movements are the initial interactions that generally make a tiny infant grin. Therefore, we advocate employing these tactics with any kid struggling to establish fundamental interaction and communication skills.

Play games like "Round and round in the yard."

- This piglet went to the market.
- Annnnddd! Peek-a-boo
- Oh! It's huge

To signify that rhyme is done, offer the kid a grin or a cuddle at the conclusion to generate anticipation for the tickle or fun portion. The youngster will memorize the rhyme faster if they hear it several times.

Please wait for a glance, any movement, or a grin from the kid to signal that they want you to continue or not. Then, allow the kid to lead the interaction and have fun with them.

Before they can be good communicators, children must learn to succeed in these people's games.

Epilogue

This Speech Therapy Guide for Kids is a great resource for parents to help their child improve their speech. It provides practical advice and exercises that can be done by the child and the parent together.

The Speech Therapy Guide for Kids has many useful tips that can help any parent or caregiver who is dealing with a child who has speech difficulties. It is a good starting point for understanding what it entails and how it can be beneficial for children.

The conclusion is that speech therapy is a valuable option for children who are struggling with language skills.

Hey Friends!

How has been your experience after reading the book?

Hope that this book improves your life, health and wellbeing. Your precious feedback would be of great value for us and help us improve.

Thanks and Stay Connected with us for FREE Goodies at:

info@hafizpublications.com

Visit us at : hafizpublications.com